AVERSE

(OR TWO)

TO OPERA

AND OTHER MUSICAL DIVERSIONS

Frank Walker

First published in Great Britain in 2019

Text © 2019 Frank Walker

ISBN: 9 780952 994350

Printed and bound by Print2Demand Ltd.
1, Newlands Road,
Westoning
Bedfordshire, MK45 5LD

Partlet & Daly

CONTENTS

Overture

Performers and their Audiences

Operas and Synopses

OVERTURE

A Bravura Air

Exactly what is opera?

Exactly what is opera?
I used to think I knew:
A large scale, badly acted play
That's sung the whole way through –

While musicals, though not so grand,
Have speaking interposed.
So why aren't they called operas too
When scores are through-composed?

There's spieloper and singspiel
Where performers sometimes speak,
As so they do in *Carmen*
But that's opéra comique.

Now this I find confusing
Though admittedly I'm dim
For *Carmen*'s not *comique* at all:
The final act is grim.

Spieloper's like a musical
But written long ago.
I thought I'd got that sorted
Till I saw *Fidelio* –

When noticing the dialogue
Throughout the composition
I said, "I like spieloper,"
Just to flaunt my erudition.

But denigrating comments
Knocked my show of learning flat:
"It's Beethoven's one *opera* –
It's always known as that."

I wish they'd make their minds up
In the way these terms are used.
Such sloven inconsistency
Is getting me confused.

I recognize that Franz Léhar
And Strauss wrote operetta:
I'm on much safer ground with them
So fare a little better.

How comes it then that opera buffs
Are apt to look askance
When I attach that label
To *The Pirates of Penzance* ?

They tell me *operetta*
Is a term kept quite apart
From all those operettas
Which were staged by D'Oyly Carte.

It's hard to see distinctions
And believe you me I've tried.
I've read, researched; I've *Googled*
But it's hardly cut and dried.

From Handel to Lloyd-Webber,
Now, with people in the know,
I find it best to hedge my bets
And say, "I've seen a show."

Music Theory

Musicians of note learn their lessons by rote
And commonly quote quaint mnemonics,
Such as *Every Good Boy,* which they tend to employ
When devising new chords and harmonics.

A scholarly tone is their *sine qua non*
But the worst of their maddening ways is
A constant endeavour to prove that they're clever
By using obscure foreign phrases.

Rubato, legato, glissando, staccato,
Giocoso, maestoso and such –
Crescendo, morendo drive *me* round the bend. Oh!
They might as well speak Double Dutch.

Why pedantically choose to use words that confuse
When a simple one serves the same function?
Would they drive *allegretto*, accelerate *stretto*
Or *rall* when approaching a junction?

This jargon arcane is a bit of a pain
For a plain speaking fellow like me:
It's absurd! Who has heard of an augmented third?
I have always preferred *Do re mi.*

But this is the way men prevent baffled laymen
From learning the tricks of the trade;
Those terms esoteric and phrases mesmeric
Convince us they're worth all they're paid.

Denoting each key, using A through to G,
Composers convey what they mean.
They don't need *augmented* or such terms invented
To label the gaps in between.

The style (more or less) of how chords should progress
Is instinctive to every musician;
Enthused by their Muse to write hymns or the blues,
They all choose by divine intuition.

Music is flavoured by intervals favoured
In search of original style –
Which helps us to tell Johann Strauss from Ravel
And for Wagner to stand out a mile.

But get the percussion or brass in discussion
Concerning these intricate facts;
And I'll bet, they concur – intervals they prefer
Are the ones in between the two acts.

Then they're off for a jar in the theatre bar
And with luck there'll be time for one more.
For they rate a bar's rest with a pint and a jest
As the best of the bars in the score.

Verismo

When a composer's
Opera shows us
Worlds of let's pretend,
Our disbelief
With some relief
We happily suspend –
But when they think
That kitchen sink
Eclipses fairy tale,
They're apt to find
Their work inclined
To disappoint and fail.

You see

There is no
Verismo.
I'd like to make that plain:
The fools who feel
That opera's real,
I'd certify insane.

When jealousy fuels
Sicilian duels,
If quarrels have brewed too long,
A man with a knife
Who's avenging his wife
Is not in the mood for a song.

When Nixon went
By plane and spent
A week with Mao Tse Tung,
We'd all have laughed
And thought it daft
If either man had sung.

Though a plot's jam-packed
With historical fact
The point we can never dismiss,
Is that once it is set
To a score, what we get
Is elegant artifice.

The clever librettist
Should never forget his
Concerns for what's heartfelt and true
But accept that to sing
A duet is a thing
That the man in the street doesn't do.

The best opera teems
With improbable themes
And tales that may well seem absurd:
Yet through its conventions
And lofty pretensions
The deepest emotions are stirred.

I know it annoys
To have girls playing boys,
Who then dress up as girls when disguised;
And it irks to be asked
To believe a half-masked
Wayward wife would go unrecognized.

Yet, despite all the quirks,
It has magic that works
As it draws on all forces artistic;
But we have to confess
It's a bit of a mess
When it tries to look naturalistic.

Villains in Operetta

I cannot understand it:
Both the pirate and the bandit
Are ruffians, intent on doing harm.
Yet no sooner do you get a
Chap like that in operetta
Than he'll effervesce with gaiety and charm.

Conspirators on stage
Abandon all their brooding rage
When dressed in wide-brimmed hats and long, black cloaks.
Indeed their only threat
Is disregard of etiquette:
Upstaging with interminable jokes.

It's the music, I surmise,
Which has the power to civilize –
A point which the authorities should heed.
They could free all thugs and brutes
From Young Offenders' Institutes:
A course in operetta's all they need.

Instead of doing time
For having led a life of crime,
If ne'er-do-wells were made to join a choir,
It would save a cash-strapped nation
Costs of rehabilitation
And governors of prisons could retire.

The Washtub Bass

If they lacked orchestral colour,
Opera scores would be much duller.
Skilful use of orchestration
Kindles our imagination;
Hinting by the tones we hear
At character and atmosphere.
Composers, with this thought in mind,
Use instruments of every kind.
To underscore and intertwine
According to the vocal line.
So why is it I've never seen a
Washtub bass or ocarina?
And why is it composers scorn
The virginals and alpenhorn?
The theremin so weirdly waily,
Hurdy-gurdy, ukelele,
Phonofiddle, hecklephone –
In opera scores they're hardly known;
The glass harmonica, didgeridoo,
The tongs and the bones, and the humble kazoo,
The dulcimer and clavichord
Are all too frequently ignored.
Sackbuts, racketts, shawms and saws
Are overlooked in opera scores.
So should the life of a musician,
Root itself as your ambition,
Don't succumb to the allure
Of instruments now thought obscure.
Remember you must earn your bread –
So learn the violin instead.

PERFORMERS
AND THEIR
AUDIENCES

The Aficionado

You may greatly admire
(Or aspire to acquire)
The role of *aficionado*
But it's boring to pore
Over notes by the score
From *The Pearl Fishers* to *The Mikado*.

With Mozart, Bellini,
Scarlatti, Puccini,
Tchaikovsky and Gluck for a start;
Mussorgsky, Spontini,
Saint-Saëns and Rossini –
There's too much to learn off by heart.

What you need are some phrases
To form a sound basis
(A dozen at most should be plenty)
Then trot 'em out pat
During interval chat
And you'll feel like the real cognoscenti.

Vibrato, libretto,
Castrato, falsetto
Are useful to have up your sleeve;
And never forget
That the opera set
Call the boring bits *recitative*.

14

Just a smattering tends
To convince all your friends –
Though it's easy to wreck the façade,
When you're told the soubrette
Was last seen at The Met
And you think that they mean Scotland Yard.

If you mug up the plot
(And there's never a lot)
It's unlikely you'll put a foot wrong.
But it's viewed as a crime
To refer to *half time* –
And an *aria* please not a *song*.

To avoid a mishap
Don't be tempted to clap
Till you're perfectly sure of your ground.
Then over-enthuse;
Join the cheers or the boos
Taking cues from those sitting around.

For these opera chaps
Set ingenious traps
Which are hidden throughout opera scores,
So sooner or later
The novice spectator
Is lured into solo applause.

To avoid a red face
Or a social disgrace,
Cry, *Bravo* or *Bis* – not *Encore*.
But divas like *Brava!*
A purist palaver,
Which thrills the true opera bore.

Should you fear that a seat
At the opera's replete
With great pitfalls and not worth the risk –
Then to hear *William Tell*
Without going through Hell,
Stay at home and enjoy it on disc.

A Matter of Style

If you've ever had to suffer
From a night of opera buffa,
Remember: opera seria
Is infinitely drearier.

The Fat Lady Sings

The fat lady sang but the opera went on,
Which to my way of thinking was wrong;
And I couldn't quite see
How a girl with T. B.
Had a voice so incredibly strong.

Between you and me, if you'd asked *A & E*
If her cough was the Grim Reaper's warning,
They'd have said, "She's not sick:
Get her chest rubbed with Vick.
She'll be fit as a flea in the morning."

Castrati

The History student, who trawls
Through the annals of opera, recalls
That the awful decision
To have the excision
Required of castrati takes balls.

The Train to Glyndebourne

There's a panic on the line, for it's 13:29
And the Eastbourne train is ready to depart:
"Where is Gerald with the champers
And the Fortnum picnic hampers?
We must find him or the train can't start.
He was with us in the taxi;
Then we briefly turn our backs; he
Disappears to God knows where: he's such a pain.
His erratic manner lately seems designed to irritate me.
Henry, darling, tell the guard to hold the train."
But the guard says, "Sorry mate,
I can't let the train be late.
If a passenger's not here it's just too bad."
"If you think that I'll abandon
Half a case of Moët Chandon,"
Henry tells the man, "you must be barking mad."
He replies, "Well like I said, you'll
Understand we have a schedule
And it's only half an hour before the next;
Now I'll have to blow my whistle
Or I'll get a prompt dismissal."
But Flora's getting steadily more vexed.
"The *next* train will not do.
We must be *there* by half past two.
There are guests to greet and tardiness is rude."
A point the guard ignores:
"Now step on board and mind the doors."
"But our son has all the tickets and the food."

Their heated altercation resonates throughout the station
Until Grandpa is made suddenly aware
That the cause of all their strife
Is on the train as large as life:
"Relax my sweet," he says, "young Gerald's there."
You'd not think her quite so sweet if
You could hear the choice expletive
She gives vent to when her missing son is found
But at last the fractious horde
Is scrambling breathlessly on board
And the flustered Foxley-Meres are Lewes bound.

An invasion of bow ties occasions minimal surprise
On Eastbourne trains when Glyndebourne starts its run,
But a chill of apprehension
Grips the passengers' attention
As Flora, fiercely smiling, chides her son.
Though she thinks that her reproach
Is merely whispered, half the coach
Is clearly riveted and every ear is strained,
While glossy magazines are put to use as folding screens
By those whom Flora's keeping entertained.
As they pull out of Victoria in a mood far from euphoria,
Grandpa is the only one to smile:
Quite impervious to the frost
Of his daughter who's been crossed,
He decides to take the limelight for a while.
"I think it helps to know at least a rough scenario
So I'll put you in the picture if I can.
This is opera at its best: there's young Tamino on a quest
With a funny little chap more bird than man..."

They are bored but no-one stops his
Convoluted, loud synopsis
Until Gerald steels himself to interfere:
"Grandpa I don't dispute the fact you know your *Magic Flute,*
But we've booked to see *Der Rosenkavalier.*"
"Good God! Not Richard Strauss,"
Harrumphs the old man in a grouse.
"If I'd known that, I'd not have said I'd go.
His operas are appalling – endless bloody caterwauling.
Now Mozart does, at least, write tunes I know.
I've been shamelessly misled…"
"…Daddy, please, I'm sure we said.."
"No you didn't!" snaps her father getting surly.
"I'd have turned you both down flat
But I should have smelled a rat
When you told me we were setting off so early.
Strauss goes on far too long and my bladder isn't strong;
When I've had about an hour of sitting still,
I get fidgety and tense thinking, "Will I make the Gents?"
Oh! I wish I hadn't had my water pill.
It's a mercy Meg and Ken haven't tagged along again,
Or that *would* put the kibosh on the night."
Flora breaks it gently, "They're arriving in the Bentley.
We're meeting there. Just try to be polite."
Her father grinds his teeth,
"I'm getting get off at Haywards Heath.
I'll catch the next train back and dine alone."
"You'll do nothing of the sort," is Flora's menacing retort
But Grandpa's not deflected from his moan.

"I find Kenneth such a bore and never easy to ignore.
He's so convinced he's right – and far too loud;
And even *you* must notice
His pink socks and halitosis
That always make him stand out in a crowd.
What's more, he's one of those
Who sings along to bits he knows
While conducting every note of the event;
Yet never seems aware
When those around him turn and stare
And scowl at him with murderous intent.
You have to face the facts: we're all unable to relax
In the certainty they're bound to make a scene:
Like the farce last year when Meg
Said she'd been bitten on the leg
And screamed when we'd no antihistamine.
You'd have thought her like to die
(I wish she had); then, God knows why,
She pulled her evening skirt above her knees
And proceeded to distract
By scratching through the second act
Like a mongrel bitch that's overrun with fleas."
"I concede she's highly strung,"
Says Flora; "spoiled to death when young
And I acknowledge that her dress sense is outré,
But Daddy please don't scold:
You know they both have hearts of gold
And put a lot of business Henry's way.
Make an effort, there's a dear. It's only one day in the year."

"No, there's Christmas: and that's something else I dread.
I'll get dragged along again
For yet another dose of Ken,
Though with any luck by then I might be dead."

Persisting in this vein their stern invective thrills the train
Until at last at Lewes they alight,
Where hampered by his struggle
With the load he has to juggle,
Weary Gerald sees his family breeze from sight.
There's a sliding-to of doors
Which cues spontaneous applause
As the passengers' approval is made plain;
Pulling out of Lewes station
They express their approbation
For the cast of the railway train.

With apologies to T. S. Eliot

Women in Opera

Composers treat women with little respect.
In opera it's practically certain
The poor prima donna will end up a goner:
It's few that survive till the curtain.

If she hasn't gone mad, been consumed by disease,
Or discovered a knife in her back,
She'll be killed by a fall from a high city wall,
Or be found by her dad in a sack.

She'll commit harakiri, eat poisonous plants;
She'll be throttled or raped by a squire,
Or cause a sensation by self-immolation –
Chargrilled on a funeral pyre.

But if the composer should grant a reprieve
She's still little cause to be glad:
He'll cast and offend her to act as transgender
And spend the night dressed as a lad.

It was once all the rage on the musical stage
But in *this* day and age it's misogyny.
Those mezzos in trousers no longer arouse us:
Now everyone's used to androgyny.

Operatic Irritants

There are those who talk through the overture;
There are those who rustle their sweets
And I'm terribly vexed
By those who text
On 'phones with musical tweets.

There are those who whisper, "Excuse me please:
I'm sorry was that your toe?"
When they come in late
And refuse to wait
Then disturb everyone in the row.

There are those with their bottles of Évian,
Which collapse with a click and distract.
Do they fear that their fate
Is to dehydrate
Before we get through the first act?

And those who throughout read programme notes,
A habit which truly appals,
For the clumsy sods,
Sitting up in the gods,
Let them drop on to us in the stalls.

From all such theatrical irritants
May the merciful Lord protect us
But the very worst
With which opera's cursed
Are modern stage directors.

From the moment the curtain rises
I feel myself getting depressed
When it's clear the director
Has wantonly wrecked a
Good opera because he knows best.

When I hear that it's been *re-imagined*
My heart gives a shudder of dread.
Oh why can't they trust
Their material or just
Write their own bloody opera instead?

When interpreting works of genius
Why do they think it a bore
Or artistic disgrace
For the time and the place
To reflect both the words and the score?

I try suspending my disbelief
But I find that it's hard to succeed
When *Aïda*'s been set
In a maisonette
And the Pharaoh's high on weed.

Directors who crave notoriety
All suffer the same disease:
And think that it's smarter
If *La Traviata*
Is sung on a flying trapeze.

O spare me the kind of director
Who hopes he can whip up a storm
With the Lammermoor Bride
On a whim supplied
With Wehrmacht uniform.

Spare me the modernist mantra
That *different is always better*
Or Lohengrin's swan
Will soon be gone
And replaced with a white Lambretta.

The Queen of the Night on a motorway;
Next Siegfried in blue suede shoes;
Soon, Hansel and Gretel
Will turn Heavy Metal
With piercings and facial tattoos.

Let's end this war 'twixt stage and score:
It's time we should broker a truce,
Lest Verdi's Attila
Play goal for the Villa
When Jonathan Miller's let loose.

Operatic Point Scoring

Nothing should deter
The aspiring connoisseur
Or the diffident apprentice opera buff.
For no-one gives two hoots
Nowadays for evening suits:
A condescending smile is quite enough.

There's no need to be concerned
With stuffy facts you haven't learned
But still, the cognoscenti recommend
That it's better to avoid
Letting on that you've enjoyed
Any musical you've seen in the West End.

A patronizing sneer
Towards *Les Mis* and *Mamma Mia*
Or anything Lloyd-Webber might create,
Is by far the best conclusion
Though I'm thrown into confusion
When an opera house produces *Kiss Me Kate*.

While I readily concede
The exception of *Candide* –
And *Guys and Dolls* is such a lot of fun,
I strenuously deny
That I enjoyed *The King and I*
Or admit to liking *Annie Get your Gun*.

I give shudders of despair
At *Salad Days* or *Free As Air;*
At *Oliver* and *Me and Juliet.*
I could never bear the shame
Of being caught attending *Fame*
And insist that I don't know *No No Nanette.*

I've been heard to say how fond I'm
Of the works of Stephen Sondheim
And express a deep and firmly held conviction
That they're very clever shows
For as no-one ever goes
I've never had to cope with contradiction.

It's much safer to maintain
An unwavering disdain
For any show with popular appeal;
And I'm careful what I say
Whenever booking for a play
Unless it features Simon Russell Beale.

Hold fast to my advice
Don't let go at any price,
Until perhaps a hundred years from now,
When La Scala's hailing *Grease*
As a minor masterpiece
And the Met has rediscovered *Chu Chin Chow.*

The Chorus

When I sang at the harvest suppers,
I always had standing ovations;
And at school, when I landed the part of Lane,
I fulfilled all expectations.

My Careers Teacher said that my talent
Had made it as clear as could be
That on leaving school I would have to take
A Performing Arts degree.

At college I played the messenger
In *Aïda*, a minor part,
Which they thought would build my confidence
And was not a bad rôle for a start.

My tutor was dead supportive
Predicting that I'd go far.
He told me I showed potential
To become a great opera star.

But he said just the same to the others –
That we'd bright careers before us.
He was lying of course: he knew that we'd all
Either quit or be stuck in the chorus.

One of my friends turned to teaching
Abandoning dreams of fame
To use his few years of experience
So others could do just the same.

Admittedly feeling frustrated,
I vowed that I'd persevere,
Taking such work as was offered
To try and build up a career.

I've been passers-by, peasants and prisoners;
I've been damned souls with Pluto in Hell;
I've died in the Temple of Dagon,
Crushed when the architrave fell.

The make-up, the wigs and the costumes
Create just the same kind of hassle
Whether you go on as Siegfried
Or the lowliest Gibichung vassal.

But you don't get the principals' plaudits
Though your voice is as tuneful and loud:
You're there just to make up the numbers,
Hardly seen at the back of the crowd.

How I resented the curtain calls
And some of them go on for hours,
While that bitch of a prima donna
Gets hay fever from all of the flowers.

Throughout all my years in the business
I only once had a named part
When I went on as Bunthorne's Solicitor
In my time with the D'Oyly Carte.

I know that the rôle is non-speaking
And he's not even given a song
But my name was at least in the cast list.
It's a pity the spelling was wrong.

My teacher friend said, "Don't give up lad,
I'm certain that Fate will be kind."
But I ought to have twigged from that glint in his eye
That he'd some kind of mischief in mind.

For next news, behold, I'm invited
On paper that looked official
Inviting me to audition
For the season at Bad Ischl.

They thought I could play Gasparone
But a bit of research made it clear,
Like Godot – he's there in the title:
Star billing but doesn't appear.

I knew it was Colin, the teacher:
It's the kind of daft trick he would play
And I knew from my sore disappointment
It was time that I called it a day.

A singer's career is divided, you see,
Into years in which he trains;
The years of failed auditions;
Then running a teashop in Staines.

My café is choc full of photos
And to tell you the truth, I don't weary
Of saying, "That's me in *Nabucco*;
That's me in the wings with Dame Kiri."

I've now joined the local operatics
My training is just what they need.
I've become the lynch pin of the chorus;
I'm too old for the juvenile lead.

The Panto

White faced parents as they drive away from home,
Eager children squealing as they near the Hippodrome;
Their laughter in the back seat is a sound that all men fear:
It chills the sternest parent, at the coldest time of year.
With nervous apprehension and a trembling of his lips,
The father's palms are sweaty and his clammy forehead drips.
He has dared to pay for tickets; now at last has come the time,
When repenting of his rashness, he must face the pantomime.
He steals himself to enter, though his spirit's sinking low
And squeezes with his family to the middle of a row.
The stalls are packed with children and their bags of sticky sweets;
They are chattering excitedly and bobbing in their seats.
And father folds his arms, prepared for agony and loss,
And calls to mind the match he's missed to sit through hours of dross.

Spotlights on the the curtains and a sudden roll of drums,
Then synthesizers, trumpets; curtain up and on he comes.
A rush of red and purple and a stock of jokes well worn;
Political correctness held to ridicule and scorn.
Widow Twankee laughing in his drag and bright red wig,
Hitching up a bosom unimaginably big,
His love of innuendo is unrestrained and free.
"Hello boys and girls – hurrah!
Tonight with luck I'll go too far.
Of tasteless smut I am the star!
It's me you've come to see."

A bang! A flash! And then the stage is filled with bluish smoke.
The genie enters through the trap and sounds as if he'll choke;
He swells in sapphire smoke out of the blue cracks of the ground,
The moment's so exciting, what he has to say is drowned.
Dim kids sobbing, and the script half heard,
As faded stars from soap remember every other word.
They'd hoped they might rekindle their careers, but now they're sorry
They handed in their notices to *Emmerdale* and *Corrie*.

With empty smiles they muddle through a plot that's lamely strung
With jokes that fell from currency when all the world was young.
Dad's risen from his mid-row seat and half attainted stall,
Attracted by a sign illuminated on the wall.
He's had his fill of slapstick and of villains being hissed –
"If I slip out, it isn't very likely I'll be missed.
What a neat plan, ha! ha!"
Up to the circle bar.
Every grown man, hurrah!
Is there and getting pissed.

The walls are hung with velvet; there's a cloying smell of beer,
And dad creeps in to prop the bar with dads already here.
He holds his glass with reverence and gulps it quickly down,
So grateful for the solace of a pint of Newkie Brown.
He touches and it tingles; then he trembles for he hears,
The sound like distant thunder of applause and youthful cheers:
A harbinger of duty that reminds him he must fly
To children and the overpriced ice creams he has to buy.

His pint is still unfinished, but the man will have to go.
He runs like hell down stairs pell mell to face impending woe.
It is he that knoweth 'Kismet'; it is he that knoweth Fate,
If absent when he's needed or indeed a minute late.
Flushed of face he flees in haste to meet his harassed wife
Through labyrinthine passages; now running for his life.
But stairways up into the gods are crammed with swarming young
In urgent search of lavatories before the bell is rung.
He struggles through the tidal surge and 'midst the frantic scene
Is greeted by his wife: "And where the hell d'you think you've been?
You leave me here to cope alone and now you stink of booze.
Just get the ice creams will you? I'll take Sarah to the loos."
Her voice through all the children is a thunder sent to fear:
A warning that the journey home will be devoid of cheer.
Well he knows that visage grim,
Chances of a truce are slim,
House lights now begin to dim
And not a hope of beer.

With songs ill-chosen for the tale, the panto lumbers on
While father slumping in his seat, all zest for life now gone,
Is mentally rehearsing his diplomacy and tact
To charm his wife with acting skills that those on stage have lacked.
A song of ancient mystery is hung on whitest silk;
It asks why cows that eat green grass should always give white milk.
And father hateth pantomime and seethes with irritation
For father dreadeth audience's forced participation

And many a man grows witless in this noisy room of Hell
Where Wishee Washee wantonly incites the kids to yell;
And from this pandemonium, where every tiny tot
Is shrieking, "He's behind yer! Yes he is! Oh no he's not!"
Dad prays for swift deliverance by everything that's holy.
(Nor Vladimir nor Estragon knew time to pass more slowly.)
And at the final curtain call, he feels but partly blessed:
The gloomy cloud around his wife is making him depressed.

He smiles a fretful smile, betraying glum preoccupations:
The panto's but a prologue to the season's celebrations –
The family activities:
The Christmastide festivities,
The Infant school Nativities
And visits from relations.

                                    With apologies to G. K. Chesterton

OPERAS

AND

SYNOPSES

Aïda   by Giuseppe Verdi and Antonio Ghislanzoni

How do you solve a problem like *Aïda*?
How do you stage a show on such a scale?
How do you hope to pay a cast of thousands
Without your company ending in debtors' jail?

How can you ever do it on a shoestring?
How can you make a sponsor understand
When hate mail comes in waves
To your Ethiopian slaves
Telling them blacked-up faces should be banned?

Oh, how do you solve a problem like *Aïda*?
Cancel and get *The Sound of Music* planned!

With apologies to Oscar Hammerstein II

The Bartered Bride

by Bedrich Smetana and Karel Sabina

Several things I can't abide
Like tapeworms in formaldehyde,
Sindy Dolls – and cyanide;
Those plasma screens a furlong wide
And handbags made of ostrich hide;
Great lumps in custard; hair that's dyed,
Then spiked like one electrified;
The cloying smell (that spray can't hide)
Which clings to clothes when food is fried:
Grimm's fairy tales when Disneyfied;
That tireless, comic coach tour guide
Whose well of jokes is never dried,
Who yells (though over-amplified)
From Camberwell to Ambleside;
The dentist saying, "Open wide;"
Those silent skateboarders who glide
Then squeal with mirth when they collide;
The stomach-churning fairground ride
That parted me from my inside;
The bagpipes, lard and fratricide;
And to this list I think that I'd
Add tedious rhyme schemes once applied
Whose tyranny can't be defied
But keeps the writer firmly tied
To lines where sense begins to slide
With syntax blithely cast aside
And idioms turned down-upside;

Where syllables are made t'elide
In order to be versified,
Which critics naturally, deride
With sneering jibes and comments snide.

But just as forced and falsified
Is Smetana's *The Bartered Bride.*
Opinions here may well divide –
Devoted fans will doubtless chide
To hear their hero's work decried
By criticisms here implied
Insisting that they're satisfied
With music that's so jollified,
It fills the Czechs with national pride.
They will not have him vilified –
But let me here at once confide,
I find my patience sorely tried
By operatic countryside
Where rural life's transmogrified
And pastorally prettified:
Where smells are banished, dung's denied;
The putrid air is purified.
Here peasants blissfully reside
In poverty that's glorified.
Though penniless, they're all supplied
With clothing strangely unified,
Which haute couturiers provide
In colours strictly specified
That none may clash. They've all complied
So perfect patterns coincide.
Indeed it has me mystified

That none could plough or reap or ride:
They're clean, pristine and dignified,
With plaited hair in ribbons tied;
Their make-up skilfully applied,
All rosy-cheeked and starry-eyed.
In choruses they nimbly stride
For choreographers preside
O'er every move – and woe betide
The serf whose joints are calcified:
They're made to dance all folkified
(Bohemian-cum-Morris side)
And slap and clap all flabby thighed.
I think my nausea's justified.
When threatened with *The Bartered Bride,*
I must admit I've often lied.
With feigned sincerity, I've sighed
And unconvincingly replied,
 "Oh dear, that night I'm occupied."
Then wracked with guilt and mortified,
I've had to run to earth and hide.

The Beggar's Opera by John Gay and Johann Pepusch

The Beggar's Opera was cleverly written
Though Benjamin Britten was not very smitten.
The score it appears caused him deep irritation
And so he embarked upon new orchestration.

He was drawn to the piece which was written by Gay...
I don't think there's anything more I need say.

La Bohème and Madama Butterfly

by Giacomo Puccini and Luigi Illica & Giuseppe Giacosa

La Bohème and *Butterfly*
Are operas that make me cry;
And when the final curtain falls
You'll find me sobbing in the stalls:
My sense of calm composure lost,
Thinking what my ticket cost.

The Breasts of Tiresias

by Francis Poulenc and Guillaume Apollinaire

Apollinaire caused a to do
With Thérèse and her face painted blue.
Her frock failed to suit
With its monkeys and fruit –
But her breasts quite impressed when they flew.

With picturesque paraphernalia
Of partially airborne mammalia,
It's the first of the shows
Poulenc chose to compose –
But it turned out a box-office failia.

Carmen

by Georges Bizet and Henri Meilhac & Ludovic Halévy

They say that life was cosy
For Don José in Seville,
Till the day he met a floozie
When it quickly went downhill.
Had he been a bit more choosy,
Just a touch more circumspect,
He'd have married his Michaela
And been happy I expect.

At first he saw no harm in
Carmen's eagerness to flirt:
His head awhirl with the gypsy girl
In her swirl of crimson skirt.
As she danced the habanera
Ever nearer he could tell,
From her manner so seductive,
He'd be fucked if all went well.

She fluttered luscious eyelashes;
She flashed her fiery eyes;
With flattery pernicious
She seduced him with her lies.
Though the girl was meretricious
He admired her castanets
And the fact that factory girls could offer
Cut price cigarettes.

Since the day when he enlisted
He'd not lusted quite like this
And were Carmen to be trusted
He'd be lost in lasting bliss;
But too late he learned his lesson
For that loose and lissome whore
Left the lad, alas, in favour
Of a louche toreador.

It was difficult to swallow
She'd been shallow and unfair:
It left him feeling hollow
In a wallow of despair.
That she'd had young Escamillo
On her pillow, was a slur
So it followed he would kill
The callow fellow or kill her.

By perfidy embittered;
In a fit of wounded pride,
"How could a lass like that adore
A matador?" he cried.
His dreams of bliss were shattered for
Too late he had deduced
What mattered more, the flattered whore
Was easily seduced.

With thoughts that veered from murder
To a tearful, nervous state,
He hid at the corrida
Growing fearful of his fate.
Though he fancied he'd persuade her
To reject her paramour,
She preferred good looks and talents,
Large bank balance and allure.

The bull fighters paraded
Brightly braided through Seville;
Ecstatic girls applauded
Escamillo dressed to kill,
In flimsy satin breeches
Quite the tightest he could find;
While picadors in thicker drawers
Came riding up behind.

They entered the arena
To the fanfares and the drums,
Then arm in arm came Carmen
With an army of her chums.
As soon as he had seen her
(Though Don José's love still burned)
He discerned from her demeanour
He'd been mercilessly spurned.

Thus jaundiced by his envy,
He boiled with crimson spleen;
From fear and fright he first turned white,
Then grey and sickly green.
In the blackest of depression
Then the deepest of the blues,
The moody lad now sadly had
No colours left to choose.

He pleaded, though unheeded,
That he needed her to stay;
Misguidedly she goaded him,
Deriding Don José.
She trusted he conceded
He'd indeed been dispossessed;
Usurped and superseded
By a man much better dressed.

She cut a callous figure
With her swagger and disdain.
He cut at her with vigour
And a dagger and again.
So while the crowds applauded
Escamillo's sordid trade,
Cruel Carmen was rewarded
With Don José's bloody blade.

Don Giovanni by Wolfgang Amadeus Mozart
and Lorenzo da Ponte

Giovanni was a busy lad
Whose outlook was perverse:
He loved the ladies; never wed
But went from bed to worse.

Impulsive; hyperactive –
He'd no need to join a gym:
Exertions with the girls he met
Sufficed to keep him trim.

For after breakfast every day
He'd prove himself alive
With one or two seductions
And on good days four or five.

A total cad: he never had
To spend the night alone
For he'd been blessed with too much zest
That's called testosterone.

His servant Leporello
Was his staunch amanuensis,
Who slavishly recorded
All his sordid sex offences.

Fresh names were added daily
In a five star rating system –
For five, he'd had his wicked way;
For one, he'd barely kissed 'em.

This aide-mémoire would bring to mind
The days of his virility
Should he fall prey to syphilis
And premature senility.

But one dark night Giovanni
And his faithful secretary
Got chatting to a statue
In the local cemetery.

Although the chap was marble
And an afterlife beginner,
Giovanni, being sociable,
Invited him to dinner.

Now few can boast they've acted host
When ghosts have come to dine,
Or carved a roast; proposed a toast,
Cried, "Prost!" and shared their wine –

But Don Giovanni did just that,
From which he'd quickly learn
That conversation after drink
Can take a sober turn.

That statue fixed Giovanni
With a stare of coldest stone:
"Be penitent! Confess your faults!
Seek abstinence! Atone!

Your wanton promiscuity
I urge you to repent:
Henceforth become a celibate
And blameless country gent."

"Now steady on," Giovanni said,
"I think it's pretty drastic
To go from wild debauchery
To lead the life monastic.

Your views, though puritanical,
May well indeed be right
But sex is not a habit
I can give up overnight.

I'll not renounce the life I love,"
He said."It suits me well."
At which the ghost got hopping mad
And dragged him off to Hell.

moral

The rake might well have learned in time,
Had he been more astute,
It's fine to have your five a day
But only if it's fruit.

L'Étoile by Emmanuel Chabrier
and Eugène Leterrier & Albert Vanloo

Despotic King Ouf,
In the opéra bouffe,
Called *L'Étoile,*
Has the goriest taste:
He loves to immure
And impale on a skewer
Any character
Lately disgraced.

When an innocent chap
Gives his highness a slap
(No less than the King's
Just deserts)
They quickly prepare
The grand skewering chair –
A contraption that looks
Like it hurts.

The seat thus revealed
Has a corkscrew concealed
To be raised in a
Spiralling action
Till the victim has howled,
Having been disembowelled
To the bloodthirsty
King's satisfaction.

A scene so sadistic,
Uncharacteristic
Of comedy,
Takes some defending;
That's why we're relieved
When the fellow's reprieved
And the plot
Has a nice happy ending.

Fidelio by Ludwig van Beethoven
and Joseph Sonnleithner & others

The Germans consider *Fidelio*
More polished than Verdi's *Stiffelio*
And think rather less
Of our best G & S –
Such as *Patience* who sings, "Willow waly O!"

A Masked Ball by Giuseppe Verdi
and Antonio Somma

If you're shot, like as not
You'll just drop on the spot
And lie dead where you've bled
On the floor.
It's a nicely concise
Histrionic device
But a choice that composers
Ignore.

They think there's no fun
In the use of a gun:
It's all over and done
Far too soon.
They don't mind a dagger:
The singer can stagger
And drag a death out
With a tune.

As a breed, they're agreed:
Of the deaths that succeed,
The exceedingly tedious
Are best.
They're unsure what to do
With a bolt from the blue
So eschew sudden
Cardiac arrest.

They feel more at ease
With a wasting disease
So there's time to reprise
A good song
And insist a heart-rending
And tear-jerking ending
Is one that can hardly
Go wrong.

A plot may be wrought
Using daughters who thwart
A stern parent when choosing
A groom,
If they'll only contrive
To survive till Act Five
And are buried alive
In a tomb.

Now Verdi had heard
How King Gustav III
Had been murdered
In days long gone by
And though shot in the back,
In a shocking attack,
It took him a fortnight
To die.

Now what could be better?
He'd set a vendetta
And get a long death scene
To boot,
Fulfilling his urge
To compose a fine dirge
With threnodies threaded
En route.

The plan he began
Sadly met with a ban
Which a scandalized censor
Applied:
It appears there were fears
It promoted ideas
That might well incite
Regicide.

So faced with the waste
Of his labours, in haste
Verdi wisely devised
A solution.
His suggestions though slight
Would avoid a re-write
And might not excite
Revolution.

He conceded it needed
Its scene changed; and heeded
The censor, who thought it
Judicious
To choose Massachusetts
And thereby reduce its
Potential for being
Seditious.

At last it was passed
Once the setting and cast
Had been tactfully purged
And amended,
Though in fact the last act
Saw a governor hacked –
And not the King shot
As intended.

Norma   by Vincenze Bellini and Felice Romani

Some think that Bellini's baloney;
Too melodramatic and phoney.
They don't like the trauma
Inflicted on Norma,
Who's burned alongside Pollione.

Though its links with real life might be slender,
It's the music that makes me surrender;
My spirits are warmed
When I hear it performed
By great soloists like *La Stupenda*.

Oedipus Rex by Igor Stravinsky & Jean Cocteau after
Sophocles; translated into Latin by Abbé Jean Daniélou

The opera set by Stravinsky
And a tale which has often offended,
Is *Oedipus Rex,* whose incestuous sex
Was a pastime that's not recommended.

Some say the King's downfall was hubris,
While others have blamed it on Fate
But his bedroom athletics played hell with genetics –
And that isn't up for debate.

Because they'd been cursed by inbreeding,
His children faced problems through life.
And the King was distraught for he'd never once bought
A Mother's Day card for his wife.

The King and the Queen were remorseful
For both of them instantly saw
That the family tree of the royal pedigree
Would henceforth be a bugger to draw.

The end of the opera is gloomy:
The King's left lamenting his sins.
It's total disaster: the death of Jocasta
And him with his eyes full of pins.

This tale isn't one for the squeamish:
The most ardent fan would admit
That a plot such as that in an opera in Latin
Is hardly a guaranteed hit.

Pleasing the crowds and the critics
Are seldom the same sort of thing.
If only Stravinsky had learned with Nijinsky
What's wrong with *The Rite of Spring*.

A Potted Oedipus

In the Med,
Prince fled
Homestead.
Soon wed;
Queen led
Into bed.
Kids inbred,
Things said;
Gossip spread.
Fortune read:
News they dread;
Tears shed,
Queen dead.
King bled:
Stabbed head;
Eyes red.
Nuff said.

Orfeo   by nearly everyone

A plot is a bore
When you've heard it before
And the Orpheus myth,
Which composers adore,
Holds little surprise
After sixty or more.

There's Rossi; there's Lully,
Jean-Philippe Rameau,
Giovanni Ristori
And Darius Milhaud;
Telemann, Benda:
They've all had a go.

Their works fill up pages
Of opera books –
We've Reichardt's, we've Offenbach's;
Dittersdorf's; Gluck's.
There's one by Sampieri;
Another by Fux.

Domenico Belli's –
I take that on trust.
I've not seen the opera –
Just heard it discussed.
Like Graun's or Torelli's,
It's gathering dust.

Offenbach's fun,
Monteverdi's the master;
Gluck's was sublime,
But most – a disaster.
If offered Caccini's
You'd think they meant pasta.

I think it's high time
For a chorus of, "Basta!"

The Ring Cycle by Richard Wagner

Artists must suffer because of their art –
A platitude trite though true.
But in opera, the pain
And the terrible strain
Are felt by the audience too.

Life's pretty tough for the opera buff:
If you want to be one of the best,
You must sit through a thing
That is known as *The Ring*
Or the Wagner endurance test.

It drags on for hours and drains all your powers
Of tolerance, hope and reason
But don't say you slept
For a minute or wept
From sheer boredom: it's looked on as treason.

Night after night, the best part of a week
Spent with giants and dwarves and Valkyrie,
All leitmotif
And no comic relief:
No wonder we all look so weary.

Your toes hardly tap and there's nowhere to clap
Unless you survive to the end.
Then the worst of your woes is
A deep vein thrombosis
And knees that can no longer bend.

As a general rule I am easy to please:
I'm hardly an opera critic
But I sit thinking, "Soon
We might get to a tune
And a bit that's not anti-Semitic."

Brunhilde, poor soul: it's a hell of a rôle:
The strain on the singer is vast
But we all feel the same
When she leaps in the flame:
Thank the Lord we can go home at last.

The Tsar and Carpenter by Albert Lortzing

When praising great composers
And their operas, I find
The name of Albert Lortzing
Springs immediately to mind;
And this is odd because his fame's
Diminished and maligned.

His tunes were tuneful as could be
His wit was dry as dry;
The way he brought Hans Sachs to life
Caught Richard Wagner's eye –
But now his shows are rarely shown
I'm sure I can't think why.

Although his *Tsar and Carpenter*
Brought Lortzing huge success,
When German opera managements
Produced it to excess,
The more that people saw the work,
They more they liked it less.

They'd thronged to hear *Der Wildschütz*
And *The Opera Rehearsal*
But tastes have lately undergone
A radical reversal.
Now audiences flock instead
To hear *Im Weißen Rössl*.

Besides eleven children
To perpetuate his name,
Producing eighteen operas
Should have guaranteed him fame
But Lortzing's wasn't lasting.
Changing fashion's much to blame.

Like other fine composers,
Finding favour in his day
He cornered comic opera –
 A genius in his way
And this is odd because he's now
Considered dépassé.

"I weep for you," a critic said;
"I deeply sympathise."
With patronizing comments
And conferring second prize,
He labelled him *clodhopping*
Which assured a prompt demise.

It seems a shame that such remarks
Should seal poor Lortzing's fate:
Despite a reputation
Once unquestionably great,
The list of Lortzing's listeners
Is lessening of late.

The time has come to organize
Petitions and complain
That festivals can often be
Too snobbishly arcane:
There's still a place for operas
Which merely entertain.

Though Lortzing's *Tsar and Carpenter*
Enjoyed a pleasant run,
Audiences nowadays
Are missing all the fun
And this is scarcely odd because
It's hardly ever done.

With apologies to Lewis Carroll

A Theatrical Marriage

Divorce is not uncommon in this modern day and age,
Especially for those who make a living on the stage.
On tours away from home, it's not unknown for eyes to wander:
Absence, sadly, does not always make the heart grow fonder.

The notable exception to this disappointing trend,
Is one ecstatic union that's destined not to end.
Side by side, through thick and thin for many, many years
They've shared each other's triumphs and dried each other's tears.

Together, facing first night nerves and sometimes hostile press,
They compliment each other and enjoy their joint success.
Their marriage breaks all records, though you'd never hear them brag;
That cosy reassurance is the charm of Cav and Pag.

Yevgeny Onegin   by Piotr Tchaikovsky and
                     Konstantin Shilovsky (after Pushkin)

Yevgeny, whom some call Eugène
Was one of the sourest of men:
His hopes of Nirvana
With poor Tatyana
Were lost when he shot his pal Len.

Thomas Arne

PRIMA LA MUSICA

Thomas Arne

Some composers quite unfairly
Get an airing all too rarely;
Lauded once with great respect,
They languish now in cruel neglect.
Such is Thomas Arne, I fear,
Who's brought to mind but once a year
When every loyal promenader
Sings with patriotic ardour
Alfred's stirring, grand finale –
Looking like a proper Charlie.
Decked in red and white and blue
They've stood since morning in the queue
Nursing hopes of being seen
On Grandma's television screen;
Coming home, they'll be rewarded
By the concert she's recorded:
Living it again – unless
Poor Gran forgot which knob to press.
With any luck they'll watch with Gran as
Bobbing in a sea of banners,
Relishing the final fling
They wave their flags; they loudly sing
And proudly join the chorus part
Which everybody knows by heart.
As *Rule Britannia* completes
A repertoire of rousing treats,
The promenaders love to show
Their gratitude fortissimo.

You can't imagine *Rule Britannia*
Missing from *The Last Night* can ya?
(If *that* rhyme's earned opprobrium,
I'll warn you now: there's worse to come.
Where scansion's scant and rhymes are forced
Ye Literati, fear the worst.)

But I digress. It's always striking
How this music's to their liking.
Such approval might suggest
It's high time we should hear the rest
Of Thomas Arne's fine compositions
Independent of traditions.
Let us celebrate the works he's
Famous for like *Artaxerxes;*
If his tunes can raise the roof,
Why need we look for further proof
That there's undoubtedly a call
For Arne beyond the Albert Hall?

Alban Berg

Mozart was classical,
Handel baroque
Wagner romantic;
Berg was a shock.
The waves of emotion
In opera are tidal
But after Berg's *Lulu*
We're all suicidal.
The story's depressing
The music's severe:
For light entertainment
You'd better steer clear.

Hector Berlioz

When Kemble went to Paris, with his fellow actor Kean,
To show the French that Shakespeare's far more fun than dull Racine,
Their greatest fan was Berlioz, whose boundless admiration
Was noticed by his closest friends and caused much speculation.

"Berlioz, who rarely goes alone to see a play,
Is off again to *Hamlet*: he can hardly keep away.
I find his thirst for Shakespeare almost comically absurd.
It's done in English too and Hector barely speaks a word."

"Mais non, this strange phenomenon is far from complicated.
The truth, mon brave, is obvious: the boy's infatuated.
Ophelia not Hamlet, is the real reason why:
That actress Hattie Smithson has delighted Hector's eye."

Now Hattie played Ophelia to critical acclaim:
She'd captivated Paris and set Hector's heart aflame.
He lost his head completely to the girl's dramatic art
And cursed the seats and footlights which were keeping them apart.

"My love for her is futile," Hector thought, "for every night
I sit in dull obscurity while she is in the light.
I'd meet her at the stage door but there's always such a crowd
And visits to the dressing room from strangers aren't allowed."

"The fact I don't speak English is an added complication,"
(He'd understood the play from having read a French translation.)
"But when," he sighed, "I fell to such perusal of her face,
I recognized her depth of soul, humanity and grace.

I'd see no point in life at all should Harriet refuse
To be my constant guiding star, my helpmate and my muse.
The thought of life without her is a thought which disconcerts;
I need her inspiration and her skill at ironing shirts."

Acquaintances became concerned to see him melancholic.
"That woman's not for you," they said: "we hear she's alcoholic.
You hardly speak her language, Berlioz: don't be a chump.
She's totally unsuitable: she's Protestant and plump."

His undeclared devotion was now driving him insane,
"I'll send her chocolate truffles or a bottle of Champagne.
A bunch of roses might, perhaps, express my feelings better –
Or simpler still and cheaper, I'll sit down and write a letter."

He set his thoughts on paper, which the girl chose to ignore;
As she repelled each letter, he dashed off a dozen more.
Such harassment caused Hattie, to be fearful when alone
And eager for the theatre to hire a chaperone.

His fervid importunity left Harriet unnerved
But little did she know, her every movement was observed.
He'd bought a flat nearby to spy whenever she went walking:
A flat from which a curtain twitcher might succeed in stalking.

Eventually he told himself, "If letters go unread,
I'll have to write a full orchestral symphony instead.
With one concerted effort, I'm convinced I'll win her hand.
My music has a force she won't find easy to withstand."

It worked and she accepted but with motives far from pure:
She thought, "As Madame Berlioz, my future is secure.
His star's in the ascendant whereas mine is in decline;
He might be unattractive but his music is divine."

Hector was ecstatic that he finally could marry her
And promised he would try to overcome the language barrier.
They wasted very little time and quickly named the day;
The banns were read and then they wed in Rue Saint-Honoré.

Hattie lived in luxury as Hector's fortunes soared
But soon became embittered, deeply envious and bored.
A yearning for her former fame began now to affect her
Which caused a rift, ill-tempered tiffs and fisticuffs with Hector.

One day when Hattie flew into another violent rage,
She flounced out shouting, "Damn you! I'm returning to the stage!"
"Get you to your mummery," cried Hector. "Furthermore,
Dear Hattie, you're a fattie!" and with that he slammed the door.

Despite his wife's trajectory from acting tour de force
To marriage of convenience, estrangement then divorce,
Good Berlioz was anxious to remain the perfect gent,
So promised her the wherewithal to pay her weekly rent.

With faded talent, Hattie's hopes to act were swept aside:
She grew morose, more adipose then comatose and died.
In Hector's troubled breast conflicting feelings now had stirred:
The cash he'd save on rent was spent on having her interred.

Some years passed by; then Hector to his utmost consternation
Heard whispers of a most disturbing planning application:
An architect, suggesting that Montmartre be updated,
Had earmarked Hattie's cemetery to be obliterated.

With thoughts of desecration giving Hector quite a turn,
He sought the parish sexton to express his grave concern,
"They're flattening the cemetery: it's therefore only fitting,
Lest bailiffs should evict her, that we organize a flitting.

It's all so disrespectful but I'm quite prepared to pay
A lease for her to rest in peace, at least till Judgement Day.
So goodman delver," Hector said, "it may be merely rumour,
But better safe than sorry: I'd be glad if you'd exhume her."

With Trojan effort and a spade, the sexton dug as bid
Until his hard travail exposed and cracked the coffin lid,
When Hector was aghast to find that years beneath the clay
Had left his wife a prey for worms and putrid with decay.

The sexton was accustomed to such gruesome sights no doubt,
While Hector grew more squeamish as the corpse was lifted out;
He rolled his eyes to Heaven, feeling suddenly much colder
Then gasped as Hattie's rotting head rolled sharply from her shoulder.

The sexton said, "I'm sorry: that does happen now and then.
Just give me half a minute and I'll stick it on again."
But Hector gazed at Hattie, now alas decapitated:
"I lost my head for you," he said; "now you've reciprocated."

Gaetano Donizetti

Although lamenting bitterly
His being born in Italy
Signor Donizetti
Nonetheless wrote operas prettily –
Provided other nations
Provided inspirations.

Mrs Donizetti
Preparing their spaghetti
Said, "Mio tesorino,
I think that your libretti
Are so much better written
When they've not been set in Britain.

I urge you to forget
Any plot that might be set
In those islands you're so fond of
Where it's miserable and wet.
My dear it's such an error
To favour Inghilterra.

No one but a fool
Would set a show in Liverpool:
Your *Emily the Scouse,*
Despite a fine, averted duel,
Would surely be much better
Set in Bari or Barletta.

Lucia di Lammermoor:
Another dreadful bore –
While Gozzi and Goldoni
Are fine authors you ignore.
They'd both provide a plot
With far more fun that Walter Scott.

Your operas of Queen Bess
And Mary Stuart, I confess
Are very dull affairs indeed
Which thrill me even less.
I like to see queens wedded
Not white-leaded or beheaded.

I've tried to be polite
Regarding everything you write
But Ann Boleyn and Henry
Get me feeling so uptight –
I fear I'll be much ruder
If I'm faced with one more Tudor.

Our land of cappuccino
And *Poppa Piccolino*
Has so much more to offer
So *please* write something *we* know."
(Those views although simplistic
Are a touch anachronistic.)

"Let's have another story
Like *L'Elisir d'Amore:*
It's sunny, entertaining –
It's not serious or gory.
I like your operas best
When I don't go home depressed."

"Oh mia cara sposa,"
He replied, "please don't impose a
Restriction on the subjects
I should set as a composer.
I'll bear in mind, when choosing,
You'd prefer something amusing.

Perhaps I ought to mention
That it's long been my intention
To set Ruffini's story
Of an old man on the pension
Who, lusting for a bride,
Finds he's taken for a ride.

It's Italian; it's slight,
There's not an Englishman in sight;
If you're certain that *commedia*
Continues to delight,
I'll say, *Ciao* to Walter Raleigh;
Benvenuto, Don Pasquale!"

George Frideric Handel

The King asked
The Queen, and
The Queen asked
The Chamberlain,
"Could we have some music
For the Royal River Cruise?"
The Queen asked
The Chamberlain,
The Chamberlain
Said, "Certainly,
I'll have a word with Handel
To get chatting to his Muse."

The Chamberlain
Bowed deeply
And went and spoke
To Handel;
He told the chap verbatim
What Her Majesty had said
And Handel
Answered peevishly,
"You'd better tell
Her Majesty
That many people nowadays
Like William Croft instead."

The Chamberlain
Said, "Fancy!"
But Handel
Was quite adamant
He bowed before
The Chamberlain
And said, "It isn't done
To have the King of England
Cavorting on a river cruise
Accompanied by music
He's commissioned
From a Hun."

The Chamberlain
Said, "Handel,
Like all good
Hanoverians,
The King would like
Some music
To recall his native land."
But Handel answered tartly,
"In all of my experience,
No-one really listens
So I'm sure he'll
Understand."

The Chamberlain
Said, "Dear, dear!"
And went to Her Majesty;
He bowed before the Queen
And stammered,
"Ma'am, it would appear
That Handel is reluctant
To waste his time on music
Which everyone
Will chatter through
And very few
Will hear."

The Queen said,
"Oh !"
And went to His Majesty,
"Talking of the music for
One's Royal River Cruise,
Many people
Gossip while
An orchestra's
Performing.
Is there not another
Entertainment
One could choose?"

The King said, "Verflixt !"
And then he said,
"Und zugenäht!"
The King sobbed, "Du liebe Zeit!"
And gurgled in his throat.
"Nobody,"
He whimpered,
"Could call me
A fussy man;
I *only* want
A little bit of music
For my boat."

The Queen said,
"There, there!"
And went to
The Chamberlain;
The Chamberlain
Said, "There, there!
I'll reason with the man."
Handel said,
"There, there!
I didn't really mean it.
I'm sure it will be jollier
Than the birthday of Queen Anne."

The band learned
The music
And played it for
His Majesty.
The King said,
"Handel eh?
A string of sparkling gems!
Nobody," he said,
Then he asked to hear
The tunes again,
"Nobody," he said,
As he toasted
Handel's genius,
"Nobody,
Mein Schätzchen,
Could call me a fussy man –
BUT
I do like a little bit of Handel on the Thames."

With apologies to A. A. Milne

Hans Werner Henze

I once said to Hans Werner Henze,
"Although your strong views cause offence sir
And many accuse
You of breaking taboos
It's your operas that make me much tenser."

Engelbert Humperdinck

If stylistic innovation
Were the key to reputation
Then fame for Humperdinck
I think must hang
On that irksome form of speech
Where all tune lurks out of reach,
Which he foisted on the world as *Sprechgesang*.

I accept it underpinned a
Charming piece called *Königskinder*
And had it to that purpose
Been confined –
Or in panto used to vary
How they play the wicked fairy,
I don't suppose that anyone would mind.

But this hybrid sing-cum-speak,
Oratorical technique
Persuaded some composers to forswear
Their vocation and disown
All accepted sense of tone
Such as Schönberg in his *Pierrot Lunaire*.

Let us turn our thoughts instead
To that house of gingerbread;
In Humperdinck's enchanting fairy tale,
Which allowed him to exploit
All they'd taught him in Bayreuth –
And on *Sprechgesang* discreetly draw a veil.

Louis Jullien

The *eminent musico* Jullien,
Who wrote about Peter the Great,
Was a fellow with lofty ambitions,
Handicapped sadly by fate.
His patience was sorely tested
In his quest for enduring fame.
For even the best and the brightest of brains
Could never remember his name.

He'd been christened, you see, Louis Vincent,
Barthélemi, Luc, Pierre,
George, Maurice, Joseph-Le-Brun,
Antonio, Roch, Albert,
Abel, Thomas, Arbon,
Then Thomas reiterated;
Then Thomas-Thomas yet again
But this time hyphenated.

Lucien, Alexandre,
Bertrand, Pierre-Maurel,
Jules-Bazin, Jules de-la-Plane,
Alphonse, Emanuel,
Joseph-Barême, Artus, Eugène,
Julio-César, Josué,
Jean, Michel, Noé, Daniel,
 Adolphe, and Dieudonné.

This might, at first sight, seem excessive
But do not dismiss out of hand
His dad's inclination to show admiration
For all of the lads in the band.
Be grateful instead that young Louis
Did not emulate his papa
For *he* had four hundred musicians
And that would be going too far.

He led a fine army of fiddles;
Battalions of brasses besides,
Great batteries of woodwind and serpents
And as often as not ophicleides.
Percussion joined forces with cannons,
Or peas to make rain pit-a-pat;
Then for thunder a huge garden roller,
Whose pitch was reputedly flat.

He wasted a fortune on waistcoats;
Cultivated a curly moustache,
Twirled a baton encrusted with jewels
And dazzled the crowds with panache.
Exhausted from frenzied conducting,
He'd collapse in a fine velvet chair
To take a brief pause and enjoy the applause
From his fans at the *Concerts d'hiver.*

Tickets were sold in their thousands
For the scale of his concerts was grand
But it can't be denied that they paled alongside
The extravagant opera he'd planned.
With Peter the Great as his subject
And a vision insanely immense,
He embarked on a scheme to accomplish his dream
Quite unhindered by thoughts of expense.

He hired the best singers in London,
An orchestra, costumes and set,
With a chorus, whose forces augmented by horses,
Produced a noise few would forget.
When houses nearby feared an earthquake,
Jullien's show was the cause,
For the music was mightily thunderous
But, sad to say, not the applause.

The success that he craved was denied him;
The critics declared it was dire.
The crowds stayed away and the score sad to say
Was consumed in a terrible fire.
Because of his changes in fortune
And the shock of this dreadful mischance,
He ended his days sadly broken,
Insolvent, insane and in France.

Emmerich Kálmán

When they fired the starting pistol
Which began the First World War
And Archduke Ferdinand got in the way,
Young Kálmán was distraught;
He felt anxious, tense and fraught
For the chap had had a very trying day.

Young Austrians enlisted
And were posted to the front,
To the barbed wire, to the trenches and the damp:
To endure that living hell
Of mustard gas and shot and shell
While Kálmán faced the curse of writer's cramp.

It had not been his intention
To compose throughout the war
But we have to understand, the tragic fact is
The fellow couldn't fight as
He had terrible arthritis
From the strain of far too much piano practice.

There are many who disparage
His inconsequential plots;
His escapist tendencies – and still complain
That his work was too banal
But it helped to boost morale
So Kálmán's hard travail was not in vain.

To comfort shell-shocked soldiers
After weary years of war,
Nothing in the theatre was better
Than the frivolous excesses
Of those glamorous princesses
Who appeared in every Kálmán operetta.

Now when Hitler stressed the *manic*
In *Germanic* later on,
Instinctively poor Kálmán took the view
That the so called Silver Age
Of the operetta stage
And its glory days in Austria were through.

But Hitler reassured him
With a compliment of sorts,
"Since you write the kind of music that I like,
Though you're Jewish and Hungarian,
I'll regard you as an Aryan
If you'll continue writing for the Reich."

Finding favour with the Führer
Was most fortunate, it's true
But Kálmán wisely feared his country's fate;
So rejecting any scheme
That might support that vile regime,
He decided it was time to emigrate.

This peremptory departure
Put the Führer in a flap
And he grumbled, "It is now I understand
I should not have changed my views
Regarding music of the Jews:
It's degenerate – and Kálmán must be banned!"

"Gott sei Dank," he said, "for Wagner.
Let a German soldier hear
How fine heroic music should be sung."
Quite forgetting he enjoys a
Lively knees up; not *Tannhäuser*
Or a *sing-along-a-Götterdämmerung.*

Thus deprived of Kálmán's music
Hitler's soldiers felt depressed:
They wondered what was left worth fighting for.
Faced with solemn *Lohengrin*
They soon lost the will to win
And it's no surprise the Führer lost the war.

The Germans still love Kálmán –
He is held in high esteem;
His entertaining shows are doing well,
With every new revival
Reaffirming his survival,
While the man who tried to ban him burns in Hell.

Jacques Offenbach

The pitiless musicians
In the pit had had suspicions
That the first trombonist's hair
Was not his own.
So severely was it coiffed,
It could withstand the fiercest draught;
Suggesting it was bought
And not home grown.

One night when playing Suppé,
Confirmation of a toupée
Was afforded,
To the orchestra's delight,
When a skilful hook and thread
Snatched the thatch from off his head
And whisked it,
In a twinkling, out of sight.

The bandsmen did their best
To keep their merriment suppressed
But their efforts were of
Very little use –
For they heartily enjoyed a
Cruel dose of Schadenfreude
Except the first trombone
Whose face was puce.

Such hilarious confusion
In the pit drew one conclusion:
That the brain behind
So mischievous a lark
And the man they ought to thank
For having dreamt up such a prank
Was that fellow on the 'cello:
Offenbach.

The name that sprang to mind
Had, in this instance, been maligned:
Though in fairness,
He had earned a reputation
For conceiving impish jokes
Besides the odd outrageous hoax
Which conductors
Found a constant irritation.

The nightly repetition
That a jobbing pit musician
Has to face was more
Than Offenbach could bear;
So he hoped through sheer inanity
Of pranks he'd save his sanity.
A view his chef d'orchestre
Didn't share.

He had mortified the flautist,
Who naïvely never thought his
Sheets of music would be
Shuffled all askew –
Till the overture began
When he perceived to his chagrin,
That he was playing from
The ballet in Act Two.

He'd upset the German horn,
Whose music stand he'd slightly sawn
And the tuba,
A musician of repute,
Who was shocked and disconcerted
That a sock had been inserted
Down his instrument,
Thus rendering him mute.

When the musical director
Was beginning to suspect a
Drop in volume from the 'cello
Desks one night,
He caught Offenbach displaying
Virtuosity by playing
Notes in turn
With the musician on his right.

"I am running out of patience,
Offenbach! Your provocations,
Are insufferable,"
He cried. "I'm deeply shocked.
Since you've chosen to devote
Your skills to every other note
It's *only* fair
If half your pay is docked."

Then followed a suspension
During which he turned attention
To the business
Of composing operetta
And our 'cello virtuoso,
Whose career had been but so so,
Found his fortunes
Instantaneously better.

With a musical dead parrot,
Coscoletto and *King Carrot,*
Tales of Hoffmann
And *La Vie Parisienne,*
Offenbach composed with wit
Although perhaps his greatest hit
Was an inspiration
Called *Pears Belle Hélène.*

Giacomo Puccini

As the judge pronounced sentence, Elvira turned pale
Then declared, "I'm afraid that won't do.
I am sensitive, delicate, cultured and frail
I don't think my temperament's suited to jail;
If sound common sense be allowed to prevail,
It's important we talk this thing through.

The way I behaved was how women react if
A husband has wandering eyes.
The maid, rest assured, would not have been sacked if
My only concern was her being attractive.
My husband's libido is too hyperactive:
Now that's where the problem lies.

The inquest suggested my doubts were misplaced:
The coroner says, when she died,
The girl was a virgin, unsullied and chaste
But feeling dishonoured and sorely disgraced
By the words I regrettably uttered in haste,
She chose to commit suicide.

If only she'd focused on doing her chores
The poor girl might still be alive
To clean my upholstery and polish the floors
But having decided to eavesdrop at doors,
She heard her vocation dismissed as a whore's –
A slander she couldn't survive.

That my judgement was cruel, ill-considered and rash
Her parents and I are agreed;
Still, I hope they won't think me too callous or brash
To seek an atonement by offering cash
But Signor Puccini and I have a stash
Which I'm sure they most probably need.

Let's face it, their daughter, employed as a maid,
Had no future, it has to be said.
Domestics, though valued are all underpaid:
It isn't exactly a highly skilled trade.
But such is the way of the world, I'm afraid
She'll earn them more now that she's dead.

Bear in mind, this sad tale offers all that's required
For an opera. A female fatality
Is something Puccini has always admired.
Let's hope that the woman's demise has inspired
Him to write a new work – then they'll find they've acquired
Blazing wealth *and* their child's immortality."

The Judge was impressed by her bold proposition:
"To me it seems perfectly sound.
The damages paid will express your contrition;
Improve this poor family's social position
And maybe inspire our most gifted musician –
A happy solution all round."

Gioachino Rossini

"For my songs like *Largo al Factotum*,"
Said Signor Rossini, who wrote 'em,
"If you can't sing that high
It is helpful to try
To get a tight grip on your scrotum."

Carl Friedrich Maria von Weber

If you wish that your child
Should write opera one day
To achieve lasting musical fame,
Then saddle the lad
Or the lass with a sad
Or a tad inappropriate name.

Go for Nepomuk, Engelbert,
Ambroise, Modest,
Let your choice be outlandish and queer;
Try to outdo the Webers
Who startled the neighbours
By naming their poor lad *Maria*.

With malice aforethought
His future they fixed
By the name they so cruelly chose;
He would suffer abuse
Then become a recluse,
Lock himself in his room and compose.

Though he never felt blighted
By *Friedrich* or *Carl* –
Maria affected the boy,
He was bullied and harassed,
Depressed and embarrassed:
Oppressed by this pestilent ploy.

But we'd not have *Der Freischütz*,
Or *Abu Hassan,*
Or other fine works of romance
If the Webers had listened
And had their son christened
A Franz or a Fritz or a Hans.

Now Copland, whose first name
Was common enough,
Composed very little to sing –
Which proves inspirations
For opera creations
From strange appellations spring.

Examining lists
Of improbable names
Will ensure that the child goes through hell
But do bear in mind
That it's helpful to find
A real stinker that no-one can spell.

Supply him with paper
And cups of hot tea:
It may be a bit of a chore
But it's what to expect if
The kid's introspective
And writing an opera score.

By keeping hard at it
You'll bask very soon
In the glow of reflected fame,
When the critics are fêting
Your child; vindicating
Your choice of a whimsical name.

Deny him all internet
Access of course
Or your hopes will be sadly forlorn.
He'll end up in Bangkok
With a man in a frock,
Making some kind of living from porn.

Kurt Weill

It's childish but I must admit
I can't suppress a smile
To hear *The Seven Deadly Sins*
Identified as Weill.

Carl Ziehrer and Carl Zeller (and Zarzuela)

Die Fledermaus by Johann Strauss
Is played in every opera house;
When times are bad and houses thin
They put on Strauss to pack 'em in.
He's on a par with Franz Lehár
As operetta's shining star.
Although they only count in threes
Which seems to please the Viennese,
This winning, winsome, waltzing pair
Are in production everywhere;
But why is it we never hear a
Note composed by Mr. Ziehrer?
From Gärtnerplatz to Timbuktu
The man who thinks the Danube's blue
Is still accorded great respect
While Ziehrer falls into neglect.
From B.B.C. to Al Jazeera
No-one seems to care for Ziehrer.
Yet they'll happily consider
Putting on *The Merry Widder;*

The Count of Luxembourg beguiles
As does the mirthless *Land of Smiles.*
Now tell me please what makes Léhar
Perennially popular?
And why is it they always play
The works of Strauss on New Year's Day?
The time has come to overthrow
The operatic status quo.
Henceforward when a repertoire
Lacks chutzpah, oomph and oompah pah,
A spritely march or stately waltz,
A tale that overflows with schmaltz,
It seems to me there's nothing clearer –
What we need is Mr. Ziehrer.

Managements of opera, sadly,
Treat Carl Zeller just as badly.
Why is this? I half suspect
That chorus baritones object:
Fearing that they might be frozen
Going on in Lederhosen.
Yet they'll happily embark
On racy shows by Offenbach.
Pathetically, they think we'll smile
At French satire that's infantile
And fall hysterically in fits
At can-can girls who do the splits,
Cartwheel and squeal and think we care
To view their choice of underwear.
Zeller too serves up hilarity,
Eschewing Offenbach's vulgarity.

And when did Glyndebourne last unveil a
Plan for putting on *zarzuela*?
(The shows Domingo's parents did
In Barcelona and Madrid.
You know? Those gems the world forgets
Like G and S with castanets.)
Smouldering looks and stamping feet
Compared with which Strauss looks effete.
His world of weary waltzing is no
Substitute for such machismo.
Even Frosch, his comic jailer,
Can't compete with Spain's *zarzuela*.
Yet impresarios galore
Dish up what they have served before.
The reason for this sad disdain
I'll now endeavour to explain.
These operatic underdogs
Come last in all the catalogues
And as they all begin with Z
Their rivals' work gets done instead.
So if that wondrous treasure trove
Attributed to Mr. Grove
Could rearrange the alphabet
We might see a revival yet.

E POI LE PAROLE

Librettists

There comes in the artistic life
Of many great composers,
When wearying of Kyries
And dreary Lacrimosas,
A time to turn to theatre
In search of new ideas;
For make-believe to stimulate
Their musical careers;
And fusing composition
With the literary arts
Create a form that's greater
Than the sum of all its parts.
But audiences, spellbound
By those disciplines combined,
Revere the work's composer
While the author slips from mind.
It's Verdi – never Boito;
They forget that Richard Strauss
Depended on Von Hofmannstahl,
On Zweig and Clemens Krauss.
They overlook that Mozart
Had an awful lot to owe
To Lorenzo Da Ponte
For *Così* and *Figaro;*
He gave us *Don Giovanni* too,
While witty Schikaneder
Devised *The Magic Flute* for him;
The rest were somewhat staider.

Poor Meilhac and Halévy
Are denied their due acclaim.
Their hits are all attributed
To someone else's name.
They often heard their lyrics sung
Along the Champs Elysées
But recognized as Offenbach,
Lecocq or Monsieur Bizet.
With leaden words and sentiments
The most impressive score
Will fail to raise the rafters
With a crowd's ecstatic roar.
If Wallace's libretti had
Been wrought with greater skill
Then audiences might enjoy
His *Maritana* still.
That opera's misfortune
Is particularly hard,
As Gilbert then rehashed it
As *The Yeomen of the Guard*.
Now *he* insisted firmly
That the theatre be willing
To give a master of his craft
Due praise and equal billing.
But on the whole (to quote him)
'Sad and sorry is their lot' –
When good they're underrated
But berated when they're not.

Despite inspiring genius,
Librettists' names I fear
Excite so little interest,
They all but disappear.
I'd call them unsung heroes
But that's manifestly wrong:
Their very raison d'être
Is to speak to us through song.

Pierre Beaumarchais

A lay of old France I am going to sing
When every man Jacques of them knew he
Was ruled by a powerful, periwigged king
As likely as not christened Louis.

In those days, a nobleman wishing to find
A clock for his mantelpiece
Would ride into Paris to buy one designed
At the workshop of Caron et Fils.

The skills of Pierre and his father you see
Were respected by every Parisian,
Who thronged to their shop in the Rue Saint-Denis
Which you'll gather was always a busy 'un.

The real claim to fame for the talented père
Was a novel escapement device
Ingeniously wrought by the clever Pierre
To ensure every watch was precise.

Ambitious for social advancement, no doubt,
He saw that with dogged persistence
Escapements could serve as the young man's way out
Of a hitherto humdrum existence.

In no time at all, as the word got around,
That a 'Caron' outclassed other brands,
Pierre and his accurate watches were found
In the court of le Roi Louis Quinze.

He charmed the beau monde with innate savoir-faire
And disarmingly droll repartee;
Concealing the fact, he was keenly aware
That he lacked any real pedigree.

So, barely content with the progress he'd made,
He snobbishly sought the cachet
Of a name far removed from the stigma of trade
And labelled himself *Beaumarchais*.

This clever conceit earned him friends at Versailles
And opened up varied careers
Such as diplomat, teacher, arms dealer and spy,
Till he ended in clink and arrears.

His shrewd observations of upper crust ways
And scandals in highest society
He neatly distilled into comical plays
Earning kudos and deep notoriety.

The King and his humourless ministers feared
A performance would cause deep unrest.
While accepting the drama was well engineered,
They thought it was safer suppressed.

The basic psychology Louis forgot
(Which marketing managers teach):
Demand for your tickets is bound to be hot
When they're temptingly just out of reach.

Now vocal disgruntlement, angry dissent
And murmurs of anarchy raged;
Making Louis backtrack and give Royal Assent
For the troublesome play to be staged.

The scandal and ballyhoo suited Pierre
For he knew it was bound to succeed
In attracting a crowd to his play's première;
Though he didn't expect a stampede.

To get to the front was a violent race.
Such was the frenzy and rush
As they fought over every available space
That three people died in the crush.

French aristocrats, as a rule distingués,
Aloof and extremely particular,
Were packed like sardines through the course of the play
Next to corpses all wedged perpendicular.

Fetid and stuffy, the theatre stank;
Every window was smashed for some air;
Malodorous breath made the atmosphere rank
Though the corpses seemed hardly to care.

Thus Figaro, Beaumarchais' barber was born.
(A figure, then thought, controversial.)
Now the razor sharp edge of its satire has worn,
But its charms remain hugely commercial.

Caron Fils

Fils Caron

Fil Caron

Filcaron

Filcaro

Ficaro

Figaro

W. S. Gilbert

Now Gilbert was a wordsmith who, according to historians,
Took great delight in writing shows to entertain Victorians;
Intrinsically whimsical, his skills were quaintly lyrical
With witty paradoxes and a turn of phrase satirical.
His erudition sparkled both in written form and verbally,
For he could use metonymy, litotes and hyperbole.
His lyrics posed a challenge, though, to soloists and choruses
For he chose words it's hard to find in half the best thesauruses.

And while he might have fallen out of favour with posterity,
He handled rhyme and metre with unparalleled dexterity.
A highly skilled librettist and a satirist; I still insist
He is the very model of a comic opera lyricist.

His quirky sense of humour is unique – or in my view it is.
By sending peers to fairyland and suchlike incongruities,
His nonsense was pursued with utmost logical formality
And high poetic language to express a dull banality;
He made a topsy-turvy world in which there's no disputin' he
Could ridicule society and hold it up to scrutiny.
With D'Oyly Carte he raised the game of British comic opera
Though Sullivan it's fair to say, thought sacred music properer.

His mocking the establishment was brave, though I admit he knew
Would not offend if set in Barataria or Titipu.
A highly skilled librettist and a satirist; I still insist
He is the very model of a comic opera lyricist.

With innovative flair he lit the stage with electricity
For *Patience,* when he mocked aestheticism's eccentricity
But worrying lest Broadway find the show incomprehensible
He thought an explanation would be eminently sensible.
So paying Oscar Wilde to lecture New York's high society,
He followed him with *Patience* which lampooned his notoriety.
Thus *Patience* was successful thanks to devious skullduggery
And so was Oscar Wilde until they locked him up for buggery.

Thus Sullivan, through Gilbert, had a dozen triumphs in a row
Which can't be said for anything he did with Hood or Pinero.
A highly skilled librettist and a satirist; I still insist
That Gilbert is the model of a comic opera lyricist.

With apologies to W. S. G.

William Shakespeare

Witty Will Shakespeare worked ever so hard
On the enterprise, far from amateur,
Of writing fine dramas in verse by the yard
When the craze for new plays was *pentameter.*

There was no-one to equal his skill with a quill
Dipped in ink – though some think that's mistaken
Insisting de Vere was the author; not Will –
While others say Marlowe or Bacon.

Tragic or comic, he mastered the lot,
Raising mirth or entreating our pity;
So sure was his touch, making scarcely a blot,
It was thought he might be a committee.

Whoever he was, academics agree
That his writing is close to perfection,
Suggesting his opus is pretty well free
From the need of the slightest correction.

Composers, however, don't share this respect:
They plunder his work as they please
Maintaining he's dead, so can hardly object
And he won't charge them copyright fees.

They proceed to cut sub-plots; they trim down the cast;
They pare down his plays to the bone;
Convinced that their genius has Shakespeare's outclassed,
They even add bits of their own.

Why do composers conceive the idea
That the drama needs helping along
With a chorus to traipse through the storm with King Lear
Or for Hamlet to burst into song?

I warn would-be vandals with plans such as these
In a voice ever louder and shriller:
Keep your meddling hands off the Bard, if you please –
And the same goes for Goethe and Schiller.

Edith Sitwell

As serene as any queen
She sits unseen behind the screen
To voice the verse
She's
Rehearsed
With the composer.
Reading rhymes in reams that try
To puzzle and dazzle and mystify
The public,
Who are
Wondering why
They came.

In a voice as flat
As the Panama hat
On which
The Shah of Persia sat
They hear her queer
And dreary tone,
Amplified
By Sengerphone.

And through a bewildering maze she strays
Describing wandering, winding ways
In realms of elms and limes so tall
Or anything else that rhymes at all;
Images maritime, horticultural,
Rural, nursery rhyme or sculptural.
On she drones without inflection,
Dry as stones in Soane's collection.

Jangled,
    Tangled,
        A busy cacophony
Like the Uffizi depicted by Zoffany,
Mistily softened as viewed through a gauze
Of words whose sounds are their only cause;
Shaping a chintzy world intense
Which hints it's almost making sense;
Its rustic landscape rusty brown
A restless rustling taffeta gown
Of feathered leaves in grieving autumn
Tattered and torn by the satyrs who caught 'em.
Fauns adorned in goatskin gaiters
Giddily goad the baffled spectators;
Dizzily spinning them past endurance,
Meekly they seek some reassurance:
"Is anyone gleaning
An atom of meaning
And could you explain it to me?"
Endlessly,
    Relentlessly,
        The nonsense pours portentously:
A whirling verbal hurdy-gurdy
Churning out verse absurdly wordy.
Elisions of visions unsettle the mind,
Kaleidoscopically intertwined
Nimbly
    Tumbling,
        Acrobatic,
Pliant,
    Defiantly
        Enigmatic.

Merely a muddle?
Or really a riddle?
A medley of myth
Or a rural idyll?

Glazed,
        Dazed,
                Easily fazed,
The critics declare that it shouldn't be praised
Swearing emphatically,
                "Daring modernity
Ought to be cursed through all eternity!"

                    With apologies to E. S.

ACKNOWLEDGING THE APPLAUSE

A Double Encore

-or perhaps that should be Bis! Bis!

A Modern Major-General

I am another model of a modern Major-General,
I've information vegetable, animal, and mineral,
I recognize a Suffolk Punch and pure bred Andalusian
And understand the theories referred to as *Malthusian*.
My knowledge of phrenology I've used to thwart rebellion;
But disapprove of strategies remotely Machiavellian.
I cite the expeditions undertaken by Napoleon
And know by heart the artefacts preserved in the Ashmolean.

I've learned defensive structure from the castles of Bavaria
And never trust a helmet to protect me from malaria.
In short, in matters vegetable, animal, and mineral,
I am another model of a modern Major-General.

I've phrases at my fingertips, Miltonic and Shakespearean;
I know which kings are Saxe-Coburg and which are Hanoverian;
I have a working knowledge of conductors and capacitors
And annotate the writings of Herodotus and Tacitus.
I calculate my bearings from the Greenwich prime meridian
And understand geometry, projective and Euclidian;
In Bob and Stedman Triples I have learned how peals of them are rung
And dance the hokey cokey to the tunes from *Götterdämmerung*.

I'll tell you why Prometheus was banished to the Caucasus
And demonstrate how Holbein used perspective anamorphosis.
In short, in matters vegetable, animal and mineral,
I am another model of a modern Major-General.

Then I can tell Corinthian from Doric and Ionian;
Recite the tale of *Gilgamesh* in ancient Babylonian;
Expose the flaws in Thomas More's and other men's Utopias
And tell you what Justinian kept hidden from Procopius.
I'm expert in Palladian and Gothic perpendicular,
I point out rustication both prismatic and vermicular;
Then I can rustle up a dish of Kedgeree or Flummery
And speak with native Yorkshiremen in fluent ee-bygummery.

I have a lecture ready on good grammar and begin it if
I see misplaced apostrophes or worse a split infinitive.
In short, in matters vegetable, animal and mineral,
I am another model of a modern Major-General.

I've Got a Little List

As someday it may happen that you need an extra verse,
I've got a little list – I've got a little list.
Not quite as good as Gilbert; still irascible and terse.
But how could I resist? – Oh how could I resist?
I concede that the original, though generally admired,
Has suffered in productions since the copyright expired.
But still it won't detract from *The Mikado* when on stage
To add some irritations from the present day and age –
So here are one or two which always drive me round the twist –
And they'd none of 'em be missed – they'd none of 'em be missed!

There's the writer who presents his strong opinions as news,
The tabloid journalist – I've got him on the list.
And Cockneys who on Friday nights indulge in too much booze,
Then end up Brahms and Liszt – I don't think they'd be missed!
There's the fellow with his mobile 'phone who drives you half insane
With strident conversations that begin, "I'm on the train."
The lady in her four-by-four, who's dressed for après-ski;
Who wastes her weekly shopping when she buys and gets one free –
And that treadmill-jogging, mirror-gazing, keep-fit narcissist:
I don't think he'd be missed – I'm sure he'd not be missed!

There's the self-obsessed celebrity whose conversation's dull,
The chat show panelist – I've got him on the list!
The driver who tears round the town with music on at full,
He never would be missed – he never would be missed!
The neighbours with a slide show of their latest summer cruise;
All strangers on your doorstep with bizarre religious views;
Fat people who, on holiday, insist on wearing thongs;
Composers held responsible for Eurovision songs –
And that concrete-loving architect: the ultramodernist.
I don't think he'd be missed – I'm sure he'd not be missed!

There's the fool who pays a fortune for his torn and tattered jeans,
The exhibitionist – I'm sure he'll not be missed!
And T.V. stars with spray-on tans, who look like tangerines,
They never would be missed – they never would be missed!
And medical receptionists who make you book ahead
To choose a date by which you will have been a fortnight dead;
And smug recorded voices on the 'phone which all proceed
To give a dozen choices but omit the one you need –
And undeserving bosses who on bonuses insist.
I don't think they'd be missed – I'm sure they'd not be missed!

There's the menace with a clipboard and his endless questionnaire,
The retail analyst – I don't think he'd be missed!
And those when offered cake, who say, "I don't know if I dare."
They never would be missed – they never would be missed!
The irritating film enthusiast who recommends
The latest murder mystery but tells you how it ends;
And the lady from the provinces who pulls her bed apart,
Then sticks it in a gallery and thinks we'll call it art –
And students who think tutors should be banned or booed and hissed.
I don't think they'd be missed – I'm sure they'd not be missed!

Those mendacious politicians who persist in telling lies
And ought to be dismissed – I've got them on the list!
The teachers who address a class of five-year-olds as *guys,*
They never would be missed – they never would be missed!
All cyclists in the city, clad in lurid Lycra tights,
Who zigzag willy-nilly and ignore the traffic lights.
The patriotic businessman, who proves to be a fraud
By shutting down his factory and moving it abroad –
And that curse of comic opera, the Gilbert parodist.
I don't think he'd be missed – I'm sure he'd not be missed!

The Final Curtain

Exhausted actors; loud applause;
The final curtain falls.
The stage is dark; now silent.
There is stillness in the stalls.
A world, once real, is packed away:
The magic spell is broken
And as, from dreams I half believed,
I've suddenly been woken.

ILLUSTRATIONS

ACKNOWLEDGEMENTS

The author is indebted to Raymond Walker of *Victorian Opera Northwest* and to Erik Penninga for their technical expertise in preparing the text and illustrations for publication and he would also like to express his gratitude to The National Trust and The Victoria and Albert Museum for granting permission to use images from their collections.